Paper Wings

ESSENTIAL POETS SERIES 215

Guernica Editions Inc. acknowledges the support of the Canada Council for the Arts and the Ontario Arts Council. The Ontario Arts Council is an agency of the Government of Ontario. We acknowledge the financial support of the Government of Canada through the Canada Book Fund (CBF) for our publishing activities.

Paper Wings

Rosemary Clewes

GUERNICA
TORONTO – BUFFALO – LANCASTER (U.K.)
2014

Copyright © 2014, Rosemary Clewes and Guernica Editions Inc.

All rights reserved. The use of any part of this publication, reproduced, transmitted in any form or by any means, electronic, mechanical, photocopying, recording or otherwise stored in a retrieval system, without the prior consent of the publisher is an infringement of the copyright law.

Michael Mirolla, editor
Guernica Editions Inc.
P.O. Box 76080, Abbey Market, Oakville,
(ON), Canada L6M 3H5
2250 Military Road, Tonawanda, N.Y. 14150-6000 U.S.A.

Book design by Jamie Kerry of Belle Étoile Studios
www.belleetoilestudios.com

Distributors:
University of Toronto Press Distribution,
5201 Dufferin Street, Toronto (ON), Canada M3H 5T8
Gazelle Book Services, White Cross Mills, High
Town, Lancaster LA1 4XS U.K.

First edition.
Printed in Canada.

Legal Deposit – Third Quarter
Library of Congress Catalog Card Number: 2014934819

Library and Archives Canada Cataloguing in Publication

Clewes, Rosemary, 1935-, author
Paper wings / Rosemary Clewes.
(Essential poets series ; 215)
Poems.
Issued in print and electronic formats.
ISBN 978-1-55071-876-8 (pbk.).--ISBN 978-1-55071-877-5
(epub).--
ISBN 978-1-55071-878-2 (mobi)
I. Title. II. Series: Essential poets series ; 215
PS8605.L543P36 2014   C811'.6   C2014-900224-6
C2014-900225-4

Contents

Cutting Trails
Dawn Paddle on Lake Huron	11
Grow Me Gills	12
Small	13
Making Islands	14
Harbour	15
Out of Sync	16
Child's Play	17
Raphael's Galatea	19
Untitled	21
Lookout	23

Paper Wings
Paper Wings	27
The War in the Air	28
Toast to F.S.L. Powell. "B" Flight	31
The Sun We See	32
Clouds	33
Single Handed	34
Family Idyll	35
Duty	36
The Quirk	37
Guns	38

Surprise	39
And Further	41
Finding Home	42
Smell of Green	43

The Eye's Imprint

From the Kitchen Window	47
Leaping Young	48
Winter White	49
Time on My Hands	50
Clivia Loose on a Maundy Thursday	51
Slow Fugue	52
A Taste of Lemon	53
A Thread	54
Love Lapsed	56
Bill	58
Letting in the Light	59
Tree	61
Field Work	63
Cortez Island	64
The Journey In	65
Something Tangible	70

Learning Walking

The Tent	73
Points North	75
Ars Poetica	77
Shadows	78
Tango	80
Let the River Speak	81

Arctic Twilight	83
Arctic Hare	84
Measurement	85
Leidy Glacier – Greenland	86
Walker Glacier	87
The Ice Is Going	89

Silent Retreat
Silent Retreat	93

ACKNOWLEDGEMENTS	97
ABOUT THE AUTHOR	99

Cutting Trails

Dawn Paddle on Lake Huron

Before the wind so much as shivers the bay
I'm out in my quick yellow kayak
cutting trails through the reflected sky
                        bent on everything;
silence, light and big water,
        the seeable clearness of under,
               the slip-shod tongues of rubbled stone,
the green reach into shadowed boulders.

Some undercurrent of the lake's body always alive
quivers on the crooked field of stones beneath my bow.

                   I drift, seabird idle,
summoned beyond myself, restless for the never end,
the spine and flex in the mind,
                        the inside-out of water,
the sedges, the silt and swimming things.
                           Put me inside that too.
The gills, the cyclopic eye and the still mouth.

Grow Me Gills

Georgian Bay rocks at high noon,
boat-bending inside the jubilant wind.
              My kayak sky-hops the rollers' rubato,
a sea gypsy, blown off course
                      singing a blue tale to water's bell.
Blue is this day's silky temple.
                      Blue's clerestory hill of waves.

I break with the smack-dab rock of the world,
dream me
      an underwater tribe, grow gills,
paddle with fins.
                It's all in the hips they say.
Kayak-skin, hip and knee.

Small

The towering headland
I'm paddling for
shrinks
when the ferry swans out of the bay –
a moon descending
over Manitoulin.
The swells lift me.
I climb and climb,
a tinker toy beside its whiteness.
Beside it, far seems close.

Making Islands

Shore waves flatten then suck clean
rippling hoops of tiered turquoise.

I drop belly-down, eyes side-wise,
ear to dolomite.
               An island swims
into my upturned fist. Spiky pines,
square-masted, anchored on open-ended rocks
the colour of skin or thin water
root now in the seams and fissures
of life-lines, my finger digits askew.

        Coup d'oeil
loitering on the rim and shimmer of things
holding the world together
                  in a nest of knuckles.

Harbour

Some days, I'm the painted fish wind-socking the sky,
rainbow scales gut-full of breezy eloquence.
Foolish. When the wind changes, I'm out of puff.

                        When evening comes,
the fish swims inside sunset's cool utterance –
a wind-dropped slur over the *ka-ronk, ka-ronk*
of rasping geese, tracking in solitude the Alvar sands. Why,
when peace descends in muttered prayer among the firs,
do the gulls raise Cain?

                Fade to black.
Unmasked by night, lamplight rivets
my windowed, moon-face gape; stiff eyes stare back.

                    I'm glad for the old couple's boat
puttering to berth, their red and green running lights
doubled in my hair – a bowline to reef me in,
as night lends shadows strange to stars
and forests walk.
        Alone,
I spiral through animal dark,
                    find harbour only in the rising sun.

Out of Sync

Waking, against our will,
   to cycles out of synch,
winter losing its bite, or
   biting in the wrong places.
Mistimed migrations.
   The North Pole swimming
                      in blue soup.

August afternoons
   clouds of Monarchs would lift and land,
sipping nectar from sunflowers and lavender spears.
                               Not this year.

On moonless nights I fear
   we are cratering this overheated world.
Like gods we stride the Earth with clamped hearts,
   angling
       for immortality before our prime.

Child's Play

The sun vanishes by quarters beneath the lip of day,
hurls a rainbow of red into the kitchen
where I'm singing along to Pergolesi's *Stabat Mater*.
All evening glass tumblers have been growing
elliptical moons on the countertop.
Moons lapping the shores of moons.
Don't set yet, I holler, bolting out the door,
pencil primed.

                        Earth tips another degree.
I compose myself: sample a few pictures –
Pine branches sway in the sun's watery beam,
geese in the bay parade shadows on their downy backs
   like babies.
Such is evening's arithmetic tricking my eyes,
followed by the usual blur.
The rocks have already lost their sheen.

                        When the AGO hung Rothko's
No. 1. White and Red, 1962, the three stacked rectangles
   looked to me like child's play, not knowing then how
underpainting imbues a surface story with light.

Since, I've learned to lay on gesso, then white lead,
in the Venetian style –
                        planting sun in the flesh of a peach
before colour, thinned with linseed, ripens its shape.

Now in Baptist Bay, the dusk-filled water mills together
with sky's bright overflow.
I watch the sudden bloom of night,
fear it too —
                its shadow-blind-all-black-other tier.

In the time it takes to reclaim sight, I will have died
  a little.
Stars, inside the teeth of the bay's black mouth give it
  another life.

Raphael's Galatea

In conceiving the fresco, you relied *on a certain idea of the mind,
not nature*. I see how sky and sea-sward serve as backdrop
for the dramatis personae; the way you placed nature forever
in Liffey-green limbo: cumulus mooning over mood.

But propping the Triton's hooves on the surface as if on a wet floor;
hoisting another, thigh-high through the putty waves
with invisible block and tackle while he ravishes a nymph
makes for myth that walks on water. Such heady celebration

of artifice and brawn; this Nereid court so beautifully violent
wheel and wind round the lithe twist of Galatea's milk-white body.
Though I quite like the way the sky scrims a trinity of cupids,
arrows notched and ready to fly at the heart of our heroine,

her poor dolphins bruise their snouts on the hardpan sea
as they chariot her shell-bent boat across the ersatz plain.

* * *

At first I wondered if any cumulus of weather could compete
with your account of Galatea's plight. I confess I thought
of flight & consequences. Not rape, a chase perhaps.
Her expression so subtle, I misread it, her docile eyes, cast
over-the-shoulder make her more sister to your
Madonna of the Meadow than wanton woman.

Not as alive to the High Renaissance as you, your *idea* leaves
my unschooled mind grasping. No hint in this freeze-framed
fresco that our lady is hastening to rendezvous with a lover –
nothing of the one-eyed Cyclops (once familiar as a bed-time story).

Flip now to denouement and the giant's jealous revenge on the lovers.
Acis son of Pan, sleeping with Galatea on a grassy mound, his head
crushed under a stone. No blood (or bone) on your painter's brush
turns his crimson stream into living water. *Nature*, it seems,
wandered off into its own dark wood.

Might you laugh if I could tell you that my conclusions were drawn
from a book? Argue, that a mere book could never do justice... etc.?
Be reassured however, that whether backdrop or nub, the sea
and its wet additives of sky and cloud remain popular.

Look now from my veranda at day's end; viscid night, disdaining
the fixative of paint hums a requiem as it cannibalizes the curve
of the bay. Lake eats shore and nuance of pine and hemlock blur
to fundamental black. The light-struck sky whittles the trees
into palings sharp as knives.

Untitled

Fog settles like an old sadness today.
Won't be gathered in my palm or give this poem a name.
"Georgian Bay Blues" might work, but omits dawn's
fleet apricot flutter.
                    My version,
nuanced by fog's odd body undoing sight –
cedars in sacks, opacities
                    wandering aimless
                                    replacing the hours.
Is the universe headed anywhere?
No *El Niños* to excite
disequilibrium. Only ghosts
of shorebirds singing the blues tell me
                                there's life beyond the railing.

                      This self-imposed summer exile,
a yearly pretence at simplicity, solitude.

Day eight and I can't see the value
in another afternoon like today:
red maple leaf wilting around the pole, flag-sap run out.
How much can you read, for heaven's sake? Thirty-nine books
for three weeks.

Listen. This is a day to prevail. Fog's voice
full of message and intent. No need to persist
in old habits. Your mask removed.
                          The day is as it is,
and I,
        wearing silence now after sorrow.

And isn't the ripple's sigh a faithful friend,
reaching shore so delicately? Be gentle
with yourself it says,
                finding home between the grains of sand.

All this I hear. And more.
The swing's creaky hinge
                and a hummingbird hammering air,
but especially the shoals' muffled wash
   at the mouth of the bay.
How peace arrives in small litanies.

Lookout

Dawn. No leaven in the light. The bay
surrenders, straightening waves. Time sulks
and wind, pining for news of the forest's green
hangover, won't lift its head. How can
I set sail while earth fucks up, swap dawn
for the coke machine, add fizzle to the pop?

Take a hike, as they say:
skinny dip with strangers.
Buttonhole angels in any state of undress.
Let teenage evangelists feed you *wurst* and *brot*.

On Cave Point Lookout now, I'm easy
with the day playing dead. While Icelandic kiddies drum
a ring around the sun, foretelling daybreak
by the *collar bone* constellation, I'm stringing necklaces
of my own polar pictures in the lake's cool lap.

Relieved now of the close heat of trees, I'll tell you stories
about the ship's red grip refusing to bow to ice,
about possession by light.
Believe me about horizons: infinity's
                                                    tusk is in me.

Look, fearless ivory gulls, winging white.

Paper Wings

Paper Wings

For my brother, Arthur

In the dawn the pilot flies inside a priceless sky,
his paper wings no thicker than a skin of ice –
mere dot in elemental heaven.
What charm can hold its own
against the events unfolding in that killing dome,
his face tight as a drum with cold?
And while war's pestle grinds
its creed with canteen monotony on the ground,
he knows he is the hunter and the hunted
for the killing minds of cold calculation.

Who would not be mittened to the idea of his life?

The War in the Air

1.

January 1-7, 1917.
Sunny days on the Riviera, rounding out
the New Year, grant a few days to wallow in the present,
before the 'whatever' in store on the Western Front
writes its odyssey on their souls.
My father and friends hire a Cooks car for 90 francs
and tour the upper Corniche Road.
Their officers' uniforms good as a password
to the moon had they wanted to go.

From Nice by train to Dijon, then Nancy,
from Luxeuil to Aillvilliers, a lift in Jerry Gude's *Rolls*
& the Pom D'or overnight. They hit the high spots.
Canadian airmen gathering in the north of France.

Cigars arrive from home.
A parcel from Mrs. Eaton.
Snow on and off. No coke. No coal.
He has time to finish *Keeper of the Door.*

Clear skies over Ochey aerodrome perfect for a raid tonight.
My father hides his wobbly knees from the other *quirks*.
Writes up his field notes.

"Anything can happen and does on patrol."

Feb. 14, 1917.
"Went on line patrol at noon 'C' flight. Had engine trouble ...
didn't get off the ground till 12.55 instead of 12.15 p.m.
Couldn't find the flight over the lines. Dived on a machine

but found it was one of our own. Got lost and landed at Rue
near the mouth of Somme R ... forty miles from the aerodrome.
When near the ground the throttle stuck ... was forced to land
side to wind in a good field ... running along, the wind tilted
left wing up and machine crashed undercarriage.
Got a billet from the town Major ..."

Feb. 15, 1917.
"Had a fine bed and also a bath in the Major's wooden tub.
The first one in three or four weeks."

2.

Easy to get lost.
    Area map glued to a plywood board
strapped to his knee.
 Ringing the hole in cloud
    to dive through or form up in,
like finding family again, face to face.
No radio, no radar.
    Flying by head and by hand,
compass mounted on the cowling.
All eyes,
    my father stores up
the lay of roads,
canals, craters, the wind-bent rows of trees
    prizing winter earth.
A monkey
    on his shoulder
winds his wristwatch
hobbles
    dreams of kiting
where the spirit moves,
exacts
    the four hour limit
of petrol and engagement.

3.

From 7000 ft. you can't see a man take a step
or the drift of smokes swirling over cards
handed round the huddle passing trench-time
until sundown's call to arms.

My father's squadron climbs the sky,
bolted 18 strong and spinning east.
Saarbruchen's blast furnaces, the objective.

Crossing the lines, the broken land scrawls
a double cicatrice inside the idle fields of desolation,
and as the silent beyond hefts the lack
to something brighter, he recalls the boys
skating over the frozen pond yesterday afternoon.

The Bosch are ready, and when it comes it stills the jitters.
A job to do. Thread the needle through
the popping puffs of white, the flak unseen until it bursts
in front and above. One sharp H.E. bark trails
black smoke behind his single-seater Sopwith Pup.

In the melee they sight the steelwork's Stygian heart,
unload their bombs.
                      Skedaddle.
But at Okhey base another's luck is up,
his bomb door jammed, the last falls free and fires the Pup.
Two *went west* from shrapnel wounds, the pilot burned.

Then they went in to supper.

Toast to F.S.L. Powell. "B" Flight

March 6, 1917

Death in the sky is a brand new idea.
Cut off its head when it swims under your lids.

In a week, you've learned to throttle your machine,
run cool & fly in formation. Would pass on your rum tot

to touch the horizon, see out the back of your head.
The stunts you pull off, contouring cumulus, diving for joy.

You live for this bit of heaven in the throbbing sky.
Even inside cloud you know you are out on a limb.

Earth now just a place to perch. All your life
you believed in plenty, visioned the battle, not the blood.

Your chest shot through from behind, ribs broken,
heart spilling secrets into the full-tilt wind.

... *if you're going to crash,* trips the mandate – engine
full out, fly for the lines, rob the Hun of the wreckage.

Don't worry, Powell. Someone will take your place.

They'll drink a toast to you at supper
before they wipe the tongue-slate clean.

The Sun We See

A blood-orange sun he can almost touch
                                        slips under the rim
of cloud. Dusk descending in a flyer's sky.
                                            As night infolds
slow light between continents, I dream of a cupboard
under the stairwell.
                      My father's grey fedora
and trench coat hanging behind the mirrored door.
Sixty years.
His walking cane on a hook.
I have not opened this door until now.
Seen them reflected there.
This sharp turn sets my compass points spinning –
his faltering heart, the whispered years in
that house, before he died when I was ten.

Clouds

If you were alive, I'd beg you to talk, not of war
but of the sky's white desert and the birth of clouds.
One can get lost in air as easily as in forest
but on this patrol, after the job is done, you go for a flip
in your single-seater scout. In the perfect light
you could trust to your native *nous* and fly a hundred miles,
the earth out of sight at 10,000 feet, your threshold
the blue savannah of sky. Enthralled,
you watch towers billow out of a small white sack
and inflamed with the light of an oriental pearl,
grow battlements and a castle keep. It blooms and,
like a full-blown rose, turns inside out.
Alone and lazy, you reel in
your seat when a dark shadow stamps
your double on a snowy cloud. For an instant
you think him the Hun until some angel throws a halo
round the scout, rims the new-minted coin with rainbow.

Single Handed

Three weeks for a pilot was all, by the law of averages,
only a matter of time, some thought, yet you spurned
this as a death sentence. Best to believe
you were invulnerable to *archie*, enemy aircraft,
the fragility of the machine, jammed guns.
First, the victory over yourself.
Cold feet belonged on the ground. Above,
nothing could touch you as day after day
you went up and with luck slept in a bed at night.
Death like the sun made you look away
and so you practised *sky vision* to sight and type
your adversary. There was no hatred between
the airy knights engaged in mortal combat
three miles above the earth,
but admiration as you wheeled and circled,
calculating his power and speed, his eyes
magnetizing yours at 50 yards. Cool as a cucumber,
alone, your life in your hands; and whoever falls
in smoke and flames shares the laurel and the crown.

Family Idyll

When I was eight I swam like a trout,
knocked out my teeth twice in the month of July,
(you carried me home)   drowned
three robin chicks in a paper bag   cried.
                              Even so,
summer-blue is the luminous touch
                    that keeps coming back to me,
my skinny frame snuggling the sun-cooked dock
  after swimming.
Four kids in the punt and you, braced to yank
  the 2 H.P. Johnson into riotous life.
  We slipped past shore then, at a putting pace, didn't we?

Becalmed in this family idyll, I assume you weren't thinking
when you took me fishing that day   how in 1918
and losses mounting, you led novice flyers
into the heathen skies, taught them life is a miracle to get over.

Your levelled breath laid waste the day when I dropped
your trolling rod over the side.
                    Once, to surprise,
your brown shoes polished with black Kiwi cream.
You knew when to hold your fire.

Duty

By 1918, the word is out.
Dud days don't happen in the dreams posters tout –
  Take Up the Sword of Justice
  Beat Back the Hun with Liberty Guns
– has the young bloods already half in love
with death and sacrifice. "Duty" on every tongue.
They flock to enlist in the loftier war (glamour
of the *birdmen* in the double breasted-tunic,
the Wings and forage cap set over an ear)
safe they think from the stealth of mustard gas
creeping panther-like into the front-line dugouts,
have not yet heard the cynics' prayer –
O God   if there is a God   save my soul   if I have a soul.

The Quirk

New pup in the *Pup* doesn't feel the cold,
can't see the picture whole. Sights three Huns.
Breaks formation.
                    He's not stupid,
just high on sky and myth-making.
My father chases the kid out of Hun-land,
shepherds him home.

Guns

By now you say you're getting groggy,
leading patrols and training *quirks*,
flying escort. Trench-strafing
the rottenest work a pilot has to do.

The Big War heating up as Huns mass at Vaulx.
Your aerodrome, seven miles from the line –
shelling imminent.

All night you hear the rumble of guns.
Different wars overlapping in the ear.

Surprise

1.

In Psychology 101 some student *plants* rush in the door
commit a murder, rush out.
We can't even agree on the culprits let alone
shots fired, our eyes and minds so rarely in sync.
> What we see.
> What we don't, we make up.
> Truth dependent on thirst.

                        And now my father
has come glimmering out of his grim words,
(the seismic upheaval of his death gone to earth at last)
– his WW1 log, writ faithful
as milestones on the road to survival.
   A man more rumour than real.
   Without adjectives I note, just facts.

2.

Before the court Your Honour, was his a failure
of imagination or technique against the lunacy
of this close-quartered war?

I privately agree to withhold my questions and choose
the evidence at hand. The old Kodak sixteen millimetre
   movies.

You didn't have to worry about the message in the Thirties,
lips telegraphing words you couldn't hear from this show-off
cast of characters; my sibs loved climbing gates while
I turned my rump to the camera, crawled away to acquaint
myself with the burning fire.

                    So quick you mightn't have noticed,
my father's hand touches my mother's shoulder lightly
and she turns, eager to meet his eyes.
                                That comes as a surprise.
New evidence not allowed by me until now.
I often wondered how they made us.
The shut doors of our house left me thirsty.

3.

Your Honour, there is no blame for untimely death,
but the muddle in the middle wrote decades of plot
where confusion made me run toward the pain I grew to trust.
When my father died, loss made a home in my mother.
Words like, *If he hadn't…*   *…curses on the man*
for leaving this mess behind…
                                unspoken.
It's time to give up the sadness Your Honour.

Absolved and excused. Free to go. Both.

Just one more thing Dad –
I have always wanted to remember your voice speaking my name.

And Further

Risking everything at *home*
made you a crack fighter.
Don't say you didn't thrive on it.
Pie in the sky gone to hell   sublime fury

                                        unleashed.

Eyes like a bluebottle   you sailed into ether
went down on the tail of a Hun   wires screaming,

                                        tracers flashing

the truth of your machine holding you up.
You knew losing height makes you a dead man.

This other-world at odds
with your lucky angel whispering in your ear.

Not you. Not yet

ROSEMARY CLEWES

Finding Home

After turning on my porch light I step out to keep
an appointment with sleep   midnight storm-warning

mugging my air-stalled lungs   horizon a shut lid
I am the stranger riding south dismissed by the subway teens'

unplugged eyes   the impatience of their body parts   yielding
to the dark hours of pleasure . downtown

Dundas & Yonge on Friday night's toothy streets
Up on the 10th the diamond light-scape embodied between

the verticals empties into the windows of the sleep-clinic's
chilling sanctum sanctorum after 8.00 p.m.

The TV's unopened eye   black as a raven's nightmare
bears down on my corpus   coiled in a nest of wires

electrodes stuck everywhere   hair a-fright   hilarious
in the mirror but sleep perverted   drifts   turns

to traitor   twitches legs   feet *ack-ack*   Waking
I'm a rag doll   flung   centrifugal against the rim of

i want to cry   won't   Sleep receding leaves eyes wide
I risk a nosedive into a blind alley & *daisy-cutting* my way out
visualize my father protecting 'Pecker' Pierce's back   brothers-
in-combat out-flying Huns over Bapaume   1918   They hop

their *kites* over telegraph wires   trees   make it safely home
Thanks Dad   I'm ready now to pull out the chocks
                                          go up on the dawn patrol

Smell of Green

> *"Et si par hasard*
> *Tu vois ma tante*
> *Compliments*
> *De ma part."*

1.

At Marieux, they knock out a wall between cabins –
light behind rain from the west, a false dawn
under the door.   You meld three Kings and
with a grin at Pierce, lay down your gin rummy hand.
      On dud days you don't have to pray,
grounded by the thousand bars of cloud:
evening under the oil lamp hanging by a string
in the dingy mess.
 Another little drink, another little drink
 won't do you any harm, won't do you any harm
warbles the gramophone for the nth time:
Vespers' exhortation after *archie's* metallic handclap
still rattling your ear.

                    The empty chairs at lunch.
                    The lads you laughed with   haunt.
                    The end not yet in sight.

How personal is a shell meant just for you?
Small wonder, on leave the wild life.
 To forget you bloody little fool, to forget!

Piccadilly Grill in full swing.
That studio in a Kensington cul-de-sac
where "Welcome on the mat" meant dancing.
"High Jinks" at her Majesty's Theatre

blurring out of mind the engines running in before take
　　off.
Here, let me stand you a gin.

2.

Flattening out,
　　　　　　　　the long low float of your machine
　　　　　　　　　　　　　　　　before touching down.
You pull the stick right home,
　　　　　taxi in. Switch off.
　　　　　　　　　　　　　　Just as you knew,
she'd kick hard　　once　　twice　three-and-a half times,
　　　　　　　　　　　　　　settle with a snort.
You touch your hand to her hot body,
　　　　　　　　walk away without another glance.

That Tuesday in September, the war was over for you.
Before you could say *Jack Robinson*, you were on a tender
for England: the heave of Dover cliffs,
　　　　　　　　　　　　　　metaphor for home.
What you want, at merely twenty-two years,
smells of green.　　Some fresh summons,
distinctly eternal,
　　　　　　　to kick off your one and only life.
What no one witnessed is non sequitur now.
With whom will you smoke your pipe?

The Eye's Imprint

From the Kitchen Window

When the view from the kitchen window
is not enough and the neighbour's yellow brick
beautifully lit in the thin October light
fades, and shadows steal the cardinal's surprise
from the cedar, thick and *shirty*, toss
the waltz of autumn aside. Sail on
over the fence. The pot of tea
will stay hot for when
you tumble out of the sky into
kites, coiled around holiday hands,
feet rooted on open ground:
or onto the bridle path that leads
away from the barn, awash in oak,
maple and poplar leaves, feral
after the drenching rains – all
a litany to here and now
and in this place. No fence. No frame.

Leaping Young

That spring we traversed the Alberg's wind-carved cirque –
hollowed span of a mountain's hand
the corn-snow serpentines
                        ski-scraped clean
unwinding the distance
                down –

that memory   jiggered this morning
  by March-mud's bloom   my body
in freefall again
                leaping young
over immoderate moons of snow

But the woods cannot hide their winter grief –
I could pin a medal on this veteran of weather
recall its shade and flame
                        Old Man maple   trunk split
signature of rings shredded in a single blow –

yet round its feet new life thrives
  battened down in the foothills of fungi
an archive in the tracery of termite trails –

the frozen days undone now by trees
lifting their limbs to the light –
below the nub of the hill
                rusty hinges crank the children into flight
                      the swings rise and fall
                            rise and fall

Winter White

A perfectly round white table stands
in my garden, legs vanquished as new snow
drifts on snow, turns table into saucer.

An ice cream sundae sculpted
in the centre just inside the rim: its white
on white modulated by the restless light,
iced and shiny from the passing wind.

A reluctant bride, winter is slow
to undress herself, allowing
her symmetry to melt. In three days
the glacial calm of the table top shrinks,
then sinks into a reflecting pool.

I laugh to see my face in the sky.
Sparrows fly in and out of my eyes,
the branches of my budding hair a perch
for their games of touch and go.

Time on My Hands

I know from the glow on my pillow,
I have time on my hands –
snowbound and strangely free I turn
to the piano, wake up one note at a time.

I have time on my hands to play
Schumann, Bach and Beethoven.
I turn to the piano and wake up one piece at a time.
The clock stops. I drop into the intentions

of Schumann, Bach and Beethoven,
anchored in full flight by the slowness of snow
the clock stopped. I drop into the intentions
of time signatures, a metronome's steady tick.

Anchored in full flight by the muffled snow,
I'm snowbound, yet strangely free
of time signatures, the metronome's steady tick.
The glow on my pillow.

Clivia Loose on a Maundy Thursday

Twelve apricot cups inventing a sunset-flush
corolla candleholder   song of yellow edges
Before sunrise the colour only deepens
This is the utter peace of wanting nothing

When did I last fool gravity?
Hollow stem   a rising river inside
I trust the plant to carry this flower
One bud   one bloom   one day

Slow Fugue

I dream I am a small house: dark planks, bark-skinned,
seasoned against rain, my features plain.

Night thickens inside – light's fist, a supplicant
rapping on the door. A second voice declares

I am a tall house – stilted above river mud –
open to the imaginative leaves.

In dreams, omissions count. No ladder, rope
or boat – only stilts to shinny down.

I suspect the gods. Their tangled voices
conspiring against means and ends.

I am house. My pilings, true to plumb,
wavering now in water's jigging light.

Is this picture just a wet prank writing script
on the river's face? Erasing foundations?

Once the river begins to tickle my ribs,
life becomes hilarious.

A week in this eyrie is all treble clef –
someone lives in the air here, loves this river.

A Taste of Lemon

Saturday mornings mother washed my hair.
I knelt, knees doubled on the high stool,
                              head tipped
into the basin: her fingers knowing all the tender places,
cast and slope of my crown,
                       temple hollows.

I gulped air between cupfuls   dowsing soapy drifts
     washcloth pressed
                       pixellated light waves chasing stars
     behind my eyes
                       suds whispering staticky nothings
as I imagined clouds would if they could talk.

My mother always trickled fresh lemon at the end,
then rinsed.
   Its taste made me lick my lips like a cuddled puppy.
She towelled and combed.
   "Ohooo," I moaned, "you're hurting me,"
but my hair dried to fly-away-fineness. I listened,
eyes half-closed to the crackling air,
                            her hands gathering,
tightening a wide ribbon's rustling loops over my right ear.
I reach up to caress the shine, the taffeta bow.
My first line of poetry pops out before I know it.
Pleased, I profess – my hair is crisp as bacon.

A Thread

For Pam McGarrity

                      And though it is only a week
nine women
     with life stories galore
  bond like sisters
         squeeze round the table at meals
         to talk our minds
    between days of ocean kayaking.
 I remember your smile
              did we talk   you and I?

               Next year   four meet again.
Sitting on a log   the beach   at Clayoquot,
you write a poem
        about a "sea-gold moon…
                a whale blowing passage…"

I wake up to you   to the heft
     of your words
         and since   friends in writing –
this thread
        a way to shoot
              for the stars in our heads.

That creeping sickness spun you
in its riptide
     and like a dropped leaf
            ferried you   offshore.

            You wrote to me with such a sweet spirit,
of hope   calmness
       alive to all you could lose.
You knew.

               I walk with you this morning
    hold you on the edge of my breath.
              A gossamer web strung
between the trees brushes my cheek
           breaks.
"A simple grief," you said,
              but that's mine
    now, to carry forward.

Love Lapsed

I have wanted to re-live the epiphanies
of our affair but suffer now
from striving to recapture a phantom limb
gone off to dance its own tired tango.

Best not to dwell on the gold ring
with initials entwined, date scripted in gothic
& stowed in an upper drawer; the lingering
warmth of Paris that December –
sighs of another time.

Forget Montfort L'Amaury, the church
where the organist played the wedding march
as we walked down the aisle; The Five Star bistro,
our pockets emptied to pay for lunch;
the fatherly *garçon,* who read us like a book
speaking beginner's German; the double delight
of Baba-au-Rhum.

Our love was no *Nature Morte* rooted
in concern for the salvation of the soul,
no *Woman Weighing Pearls*, or the threes & fives
of peaches and pears in a Delft bowl.

Trotting through Europe with a year to spare,
fresh from higher halls of learning,
desperate to toss the camel-hair coat
& saddle-shoes. *Fifties* version
of *The Lady Writing a Letter,* circa 1665;
the simper of 'till death do us part'
parting her lips, as she pauses

to consider the artist, her quill
poised above the page.

                      It's enough
to make a philosopher out of me.
The look of happy captivity in her face,
the hint of babies and obedience. Better,
the wild October night – leaves, lips,
hands finding new language in lieu
of a common tongue.

Bill

You died, and then I dreamed we were young again.
You fed me sweet cake, spreading it over my lips
so I could taste it. I wake to the scent of gardenia,
creamy petals, deckled brown
crushing against your blue serge suit.
I'll See You In My Dreams, always the final cut
the disc jockey played to wind up another holiday ball.

When I learned you were sick I wrote, reminded you
of the 'snowball dance' we won at Judy Blackey's party;
how you doubled me back over your arm, kissed me
under the mistletoe.
I wore pale yellow net, boned bodice with a frill
to hide my budless chest, and after supper
you 'dosey-doed' my strapless dress from front to rear
and when I thought you weren't looking
I swung it back.

Earlier still, your sweet trebles at our piano –
my brother, you,
rehearsing Gilbert & Sullivan's *Mikado*:
the light rain of your voice falling fifty years
like a continuing sentence.
How you noted my name.

Letting in the Light

For Donald Newlands

The #4 Car to Ottawa is neither an *airstream trailer*
 of the rails
nor a Pullman carriage affording the 19th Century luxury
of a lounge and meals on your lap. In today's world
there is no place for the large suitcase under your seat,
yet the first lurch and rhythmic sway out of the
train shed feels just right.

There's a first time for rocking and for leaping down
the dropped steps on ten year old legs into the welcome
 lantern light.
Once it took twelve hours from Union Station to
 Algonquin Park:
the night wrapped in wet pines as adult hands reaching out
of glistening slickers gathered ours;
held at bay the folded forest, the lake's black lap
at midnight.
 And so we were transported.

 As a matter of fact, no one said then,
you'd feel thunder in your feet if you stood
 between the coupled cars, rolling over the ties,
 lickety-split-clickety-click.
A cinder in your eye if you hung over the side
smoke burning the corners of your throat.

As the train eats track from Cobourg to Kingston,
bare trees whistle up the lake's bald pate,
the flash-by-do-nothing-houses idle like flatcars
on a siding in serial disorder after the winter's blue yawn.

Diesel, this diesel, with its tin whistle and thin-as-a
-rail look, has relinquished forever the
  big time railroading of yesteryear.

Even so, it comes as a thump in the gut:
slam of air and iron shudder jolting my spine.
  The westbound's solitary beam hurts my eyes
as the oncoming freight topples
telephone poles like a deck of cards in the turmoiled air.

Air, forcing the sky to make room
before the curtain of iron kills the view.

                        Up close the boxcars whiz
by the window. I want to touch them, reach beyond
the frame, taste the deafening death zone of speed and
pulse, ride until I tire on the saddle
  of the coal-black tanker
fleeing like an African god in the sparking light.
There are days when I long for the world
  to throw spikes in my eyes.
                      This way of letting the light in.

I lean back now embracing
the illusion of the great escape.
Take a train any day, anywhere will do.
Click, clickety-clack.

Tree

> *There was something in the ponderous stillness*
> *of these forests – in their wild, torn, mossy darkness,*
> *their utter solitude and mournful silence.*
>
> — Early Settler in Ontario

                                            The spruce exchanged
the inexhaustible air for breath –
(where once shallow seas left sedimentary rock below)
it warmed to the concupiscence of its secret root-life.

Tall as a lightning rod bolting earth to stars,
it stood for plumb lines,
for hauteur, broad-brimmed and supple as a Borsalino hat.

Hubris it had, mounting needled arguments
   on the subject of longevity. For one hundred years,
this viridian high-flyer staggered sky.

In my end is my beginning – but how so?
New life as the tumescent fall out of a nurse log's seed?
More likely wind-borne, than wasting.
                                          But for all that,
a tree you could trust.

* * *

Sometimes you make up history, lacking facts,
   eye-witness.
History is, after all, the version you walk with now,
the field notes you kept once, dressed up as poems.
                                                But I swear

before another disc of moon could spook its shoulder,
   the conifer was clear cut.
I did not witness the obscene efficiency of buzz saws.
There was no honour in the litter for the evergreen –
neither squared and floated down the Ottawa River, nor
rafted to foreign markets. They dismantled it limb by limb,
its blooming crinolines toppling outside the symmetry
of its worldly circumference.
                    The last of its body stumped.

Even the latched clouds lost their compass that day.
They wandered forsaken, bumped birds, each other –
or was it me, refusing to acknowledge what the eye's
   imprint
could no longer see?
                    This sudden body blow to the heart.

Ashes belong to earth, says the stillness of trees.
The mossy darkness plants the unasked-for – and seeds
some stubborn acceptance in me.

Field Work

The sun's chariot already yoked
   and plunging over the edge
of the lake. Fire Watch warning
   weeks old now. Dry air audible underfoot.
Files of ants drag their tinder cargo, crank up
   the decibels of disaster.
What if I ignite the forest?
   Sucked out the car window from my fingers,
the lit butt. We overshoot, reverse,
   drop to hands and knees, peer and pat
beneath the pearly everlasting,
   untangle the dusty roadside grasses rim-
ming the ditch, pray for smoke to tell us where.

I remember last week's conflagration.
   Head Lake peninsula seen from our camp
at dusk. Little licks of light hopping
   from needle to root smoulder underground
in the forest's guttural. We emptied the lake
   into cooking pots. Dumped and dug,
dug and dumped. Then axed.

Cortez Island

The offshore drives a wedge into the beeline
I cling to, paddling for St. Mary's Bay.
Rudderless, the kayak wants the correction
of thrust and jay,
                        prising the giddy stern
from the palaver of swells.
        My knees lever upwards
                            press gravity
into the flat keel beneath my rump,
while friends with windmills for arms
                                  canter
the troughs of heavy-headed waves calling
to the tops of hats dipping out of sight –

but I'm safe as a house, pump and float bungied
at hand, loving the drips of ocean puddling
the spray skirt. The bow's sleek nose
parts the inside face
                      of water
                                yielding now.

The Journey In

1. Langdale Ferry

This ritual never changes
Each mechanical step in *shipshape and Bristol fashion*
as islanders gather muscle for the ramp-dash to shore

Beyond these sepulchral doors is up-coast-welcome
voluptuous summer night

I look up at the ferry's hydraulic mouth
its steely-electronic-obedience   shut like a trap
men in orange vests timing the dance
of   hooks 'n lines   levers
the release of the restraining net

Cars juice up   the massive iron plates   glide open
I'm spooked as the moon struts its sickle-self
swinging its perfect curve west to east   stars
sparking the sky like spirit-eyes
        The ferry jolts the crib
& waves' welter   percussive
       Ramped down
         unprisoned
the race is on

2. Cyprus Mountain

I once dreamed a friend slept in cloud while I wandered
  the light.
A burden lifts. The sea's polished face meets mist.

Nothing scales a mountain down to size like mist.
It slumbers still on sky's pale page, upturned

to the incoming light. Day spins up in islands now.
As if islands could stack. Gambier and Bowen's shorelines,

blotted blue, pyramidal almost, behind dawn's grey wall.
Then *colours flared*. Burn-off, elbowing up

the density of fir, sharpens needles, polishes
the hedges, culminates in diamond.

3. Unprepared

What you see   is
the sun burning a hole in the sky —
transient sky-voice   silver-plating Howe Sound —
no intermediary

Sun   an early morning arrow-wound of light

No angling escapes this violence   I
can't return the stare

I'm disassembled
  silvered
  tooled
  incised —

            wheeling inside the brevity of light
the thinness of horizons

Unstrung by this —
the journey in   swifter than pulling out

4. Outlook

From the veranda outlook   the day's little productions
are unstoppable
                Sight returns to the blinded
takes a season   makes it quiver –
                            Vivaldi
trilling "be happy" over and over

A gull arcs   erasing space
                    Trust now
the sun's hammer beating white on white

                  Boats keen to buzz the Sound
pry open water's frothy lips –
                  the ferry swans
Sailboats do the loving in the lean of wind

Listen   this sweet interlude of day-flower's perfection
will end   turn its face away from sun   gather in
the shadows –
                evening's blue desire

5. Midnight

moon
more halo than matter –
baleful sea buoy on the unseen wind   dr.fts   out
of ragged clouds   thin as snipped tin
                   nothing you can trust
                                this vertigo –
midnight's earth-hump
                   stalking the streaming light
drags me into sky's cold eye

Down here
            in earth's shining garden
                          fiery dark

Something Tangible

After The Round *by Stanley Kunitz*

Courage runs high early mornings
when the light, sloping up the bevels
of the window sash, encloses a hint
of cream inside the voluptuous balloon shades:
a hem of white I name *Fair Bianca*
for that rose of exquisite perfection, framed
now by leaves fluttering in bright pools
up the sun-sketched walls and the sky committing
blue through the maple's crocheted branches.
The whole bright morning ahead as
the last of night opens to the eye of day.

I want a success for every day of my life,
something tangible to prove diligence
and reaffirm the day did not waste in me,
evidence I'm still intact after some hard completion.
For weeks I walk on coals, fired by words.
I could be on the moon mapping a new
vocabulary to navigate by, and wonder
what stubbornness wrenches fresh meaning
on to the page, then leaves me blank
and fumbling when I'm done.

"Courage runs high early mornings"
and I wake up glad for the dawn's harvest of light –
returning, returning, and returning.

Learning Walking

The Tent

i)

"Don't touch the walls," they cautioned.
But we touched to make the rain obey
our fingers, traced pathways for plonking drips
to pool and runnel the mildewed spackle.
No one wanted to portage the tent,
that unloved spinster in green duck
strung by guys between trees, fixed
with a bowline. Leaden when wet.

ii)

Clear skies in Algonquin, Quebec City, Halifax –
summer nights in the Egyptian
Cotton A-frame, its own pale moon
under the pines, swank in shadows, lazy stir
of breeze. A Mediterranean moment
in crisp linen. A stroll in a palace of
light, lady on your arm.

iii)

Arctic technology makes all the difference –
the everything-proof *geodesic* sky blue *ripstop Tensilk, HT*:
sprung toy against condensation and wind drag.
You can lift it with a finger.

iv)

                                      On TV, Toronto
penumbral after a day of smog —
the leaden light, rising
like a bad omen, eclipses
the wider blue.
What if we should lose sight
of it all, air, light, the view
from the tent?

Points North

You've been lost in a paper shuffle, I'm told.
Flight out this afternoon.

Moments earlier I'd already arrived at the hamlet
  once named Kil – and chilled by sea-wind, humped
my gear down the shore road,
  turning left to my digs (wishing for Tom's pickup).
Threshold for another depart, this sandspit town smacks
into old growth, climbs to clearcut I can't see.
Moresby's ancient spine.   Stripped.

But this airline vagary.
  I stake a chair and sip as the day cranks high.
If I could decorate the hum in the air, I'd blow up
balloons, fly them from the roof.
        One room for Sandspit, Smithers and points north.
        A video blares helicopter etiquette,
        how to get out if it lands on its side –
        Red handles, slide for'ard, downhill and out.

Vancouver's South Terminal, a hot spot for men
with *Eagle* or *Northern* inscribed on their hats.
Big bellied guys wolfing fried eggs and hash, stashing
hootch in coolers, angling for a fight with the
silver spotted wonder –
        Landing that 53 lb Tyee.
        Then party time.
        These wild men.

But listen, I too live for my leaping heart, frosty burr
  on my salt-caked skin, the freeze-framed flight

   of an Arctic hare, for sunsets
consuming the day-bright trees. The heaped moon.
I'm not laughing at dreams, else why am I here?

A *hurry-up-and-wait* day, I've joined the *corps de ballet*
   of turning heads, as planes roost then rise,
altering the universe of sensible speed. The buzz,
   the whine. Before the heavens have time
to recompose themselves I'm gone, long gone
on the silk road of sky. Once today I flew to China
unresisting, giant rose emblazoned on a tall tail.
But I'm a northern girl, who angles once a year
for her own small-plane fix. The Bandit, P C Pappas,
or Twin Otter, workhorse of the north: I'm a sucker
for any plane with a lighthouse, skier, or totem stencilled
on its tail. Did I say I'm in love with a man from Smithers
who walks with wolves in winter and river-rafts
the Yukon's best?
                Hawkair takes me there. Or Sowind,
Fast Air, Northern Thunderbird Air. Pacific Coastal Air.
I'm longing to fly anywhere that's north and wild.

Ars Poetica

Like a low-gravity scree walker
I'll piggyback on a *white dwarf*
        a *super-nova*
        or any scribbler's star —

there are no original ideas anymore
only metamorphic perceptions of love —
so I've fixed my eyes on the sky
        stargazing
Chandra's X-ray mosaic of the Milky Way
              loping
nine hundred light years across our clandestine universe.

I want a full confession from the sky
        counting back
to when the universe was young and eager
        how its congregations of galaxies and stars
        send me orbiting like five hundred suns
into the adventure of a new poem,
        when this time, O this time
gravity gives up its claims on all but breath
and I climb out of my life into the high gleam
of a fresh idea and when I can bear it no longer,
Earth welcomes me back to love anew
my footprints in the green familial places.

Shadows

When the cloudless sky has both eyes open
and you're wandering
in the dim keep of the old growth forest,
you might notice the absence of twitter.
The till's tinny ring after lunch,
that sense and nonsense traded between the tiny tables
made you hungry for earth smell,
sun's hesitation amongst the ferns.
This is August after all.

You leave the protection of Sitka spruce and pine
for the sea, the eleven mile beach of light & light.
Sun, looking for a shadow,
falls headlong over you,
puddles a Quasimodo at your feet.

You take a photograph of this to remind you
the geometry of light is incalculable.

* * *

There's an epicene beauty peculiar to shadows.
You suspected you were lost to your real shape and name –
yet the sun's blind flourish rights itself,
assures you, you are a woman:
shade's voluptuary, flaring hips over sand.

* * *

Sundown's elongations are dying to go home.
Sit. Wait now for the faint music of your shadow's
 protraction,
your shadow's shadow filling up with moon.
This is no trick.
                Don't leave the desert beach
until you see
               how ocean's ebb leaves ripple-repeat in sand,
the same signature over and over,
like stories you tell about yourself.
You have told so many, you think you know who you are.

Tango

The tango has me in a flatspin.
In the beginning
I am a wet shirt on the line
nothing holding me up but a clothespin –
Howard's elbow grip in this case
and not knowing where to put my feet.
He clasps me to his chest and commands,
Bend your knees. This is a dirty dance.

Nerving up I parade him as a second skin
my knee between his thighs
the wind tugging at our woolen toques
hollering over the river   unleashed.
The Tatshenshini River, to be specific
after lunch.

One two   one two   onetwoonetwo –
Our gum boots cross and cross again
clattering stones on the sloping gravel bar.
He pilots me past the willows
wheels me in a new direction
I gasping   getting it
dream myself into a dress as thin as water
just a thread between him and me –
Trumpeter Swans
in a tango of turning heads
we lift off the lake, one gene, proud
pointing toward the glacier and beyond.

Let the River Speak

A little boy asks his mother:
"How does the earth shake out its water?"

I.

Sun is only half in love with night. Sinking, never setting,
it pours all of midnight's gold into tundra's till. Look.
Down a length of valley far seems close and my arm, lifting,
touches dusk, now more infused than light,
sooty too, reminding me of the colour of mushrooms,
especially under the wings of a short-eared owl
circling my head and hunting voles.

In summer's country of light the sound of growing lifts up
its shine, for only once in a season flowers
flower and set seed, embroidering wind-hammered rocks
between pathways of ten thousand herd-steps.
I swallow everything silenced by the river's spate
both motionless and moving as a steel ribbon of light
scales its back. Let it talk of source and braid,
of irreversible passage Beaufort bound, itching for the sea.
Let the river speak.

Here now a thimble of sunlight fills a drop of water,
fractures leaf, stem and veins into fragmentary planes:
a leaf-map, bejewelled like a beacon's promise cupped
in my palm. Listen. I am learning not to leave.
The polished light whispers unlearn yourself,
walking, climbing, sleeping by rivers
one hundred thousand years in flow.

II.

The land so silent and empty of footprints, only tent rings
attest to the tenacity of some, while I stepping inside
the circle of stone portals cold with time know
the sky's bright gathering inside these invisible walls
as families turn in their sleep after the hunt; but
the broken-wing Plover, ground nesting beside the blue-eyed
tundra pond, the mudflies and mosquitoes, recalls me
from what can never be remembered, only the story
a paw print tells of surprise and flight, and when morning
comes, we cover a distance ever mindful
of the golden grizzlies foraging anywhere
so that we whoop and holler harnessing our human bond
against what's alien, yet longing too for a close encounter,
the quick ground-drop to spy and worship; hardly surprised
when we stumble on fresh kill, pale bones slick with blood
in the river-side scrub. We listen to the Inuk who knows
the old ways but won't tell where muskox graze
and who knows how the earth shakes out its water.

Arctic Twilight

All evening
we wade
between gravel bars,
sea-bent streams bowling
stones under our feet:
                      arms linked
for balance, handing each other up
onto willowbanks,
                      silver and fluttering.
Clumsy in hip waders
at two thirty a.m.

                    Out here, we're sky-high-minded,
beyond ourselves in the diaphanous light.

Sun, as reluctant as we to undo the day,
casts three stick figures on stilts
                          the height of trees,
and we walk the land like giants: lofty
figments of earth's tilted progress round the sun.

Arctic Hare

Are there words for the quickness
of this intimacy? My six lines jack-knifed across the page,
to get stuck at the horizon
where the Arctic hare vanished over the table rock
and left me dumb. I need ten ears
to catch the thump of his heart,
his airy footfall.

At the top we built a cairn.
Names, country in a ziplock bag, slipped in
and sealed with a rock. Arctic winter and I
will be entombed in December. This chit of myself,
a harmless appropriation of locale on a summer's hike –
yet, as I turn my mind to geologic time,
my picayune place, it's enough: the hare's unspooling,
the flowing river of his body into mine.

Measurement

We can feel the bite of wind
off the glacier before we see it.

Its polar muscle, a tumultuous sky-high
river-fall, bisects
               the monotonic mountains;
granite gateway to the shove of ice.

The glacier cliffs out of the fjord
                           in a ruin,
fists powder blue and bluer-green seracs
into our sea-level-kayak faces.

Halfway up, rock islands blown clean of snow.

Leidy Glacier – Greenland

An unstoppable river of ice
under proscenium sky –
Unexplored.

I watch you lose yourself
in its crenellated face,
pen suspended.

What words will you write for this empty stage?
What revisions to plot –
ice divided within itself
and moving toward certain death?

Walker Glacier

I've been told if you fall into a crevasse
   no one   can rescue you
                       but I have to
I have to look
         my eyes
               drawn
                       irresistibly to the lip

slick mirror's wet fall
               my spidery-lichened feet

                       to mirror
my fall   my rescue
          my dying fall

wind whines past my ear   buzzes (the walker)
the maps and the riverbeds   two hundred slick-feet
deep   and wind
              stripping ice from streaming walls
peels
    the glacier's epidermis raw
               walls alive to dying

I look down   I fall   I
                  tumble
                        into
the blue arms of ice   hard
               as new glass   an abyss
where light looks like
             the inside of a cloud

```
                no one   can
                                river me
down     saves miles of the world
                                I live
glass-stained light
                    walking a warning
you will get lost
            in your imagination if
```

The Ice Is Going

1.

In the absence of ice
    the icebreaker licks up the briny mosaic.
Revolutions of three fixed-pitch propellers vibrate
 through my feet, steel hull gone to a thousand pieces
in the sea mirror's warp.

Only the seabirds pretend nothing is lost.
        Fulmars coast,
clone reflexes, then arrow into air.
Thick-billed murres scooter wing paddled pathways,
 cavorting in the bow's under-wash.

      I'm on the bridge, glassing
Devon Island's south shore. Lat. 74° 22' N Sailing west.
We are past Cape Bullen, Curning Inlet, Hob House and
 Blaney Bay –
     glaciers no longer adamantine, lose
tongues, retreat inland.
     Rock soaks up sun like a sponge.

 The ice is going
     The ice is melting and I am losing
 velocity.
 My spreading wants wings
    for skimming horizons' white speech
learned by heart.

2.

The icebreaker is always arriving, yet not –
                                                            its inexorability
folds distance, headland coming up fast in a single stride.

Devon's coastline gathers the flat-topped mountains in,
their monasteried massifs of stone growing skirts of scree.

Here is the heart of magma's forty-eight-million-year boil –
continental collisions birthing mountains,
Ordovician clay, in a blink, spinning new tales.

  Kyrie, kyrie sighs the dry wind. The relic landscape.

But hear this.
          The roof of the world is limitless and always local.
Look now to the port side.
  A berg trails off mist
                    its sagging back sun-kissed.
                                        The tides move as they will.

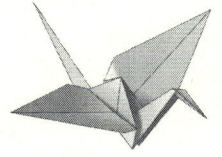

Silent Retreat

Silent Retreat

1.

June retreat. Air limping in the grip
of noon-time's shimmer. Green is thick.
I have counted 36 shades.

Soon as the question formed I knew.
How deep this pond? Clouded up   murky even
current barging scum under the footbridge

I stare down the sun's white beam
into the mud-mapped home of hidden fish –
my life a boat   rudderless inside

shadow's release. Silhouette cast over water
is my body pierced by light and its opposite –
misshapen now as sunspots unhinging

in the wet incoherent mirror   sizzle.
Only cicadas tweezer stillness.
The pond sighs   does what water does.

2.

On Daffodil Walk
                   soaked grass
shoots cold thrills up my legs
                                instep
the unconditional return to the vocabulary of bones.
Learning walking.
                   Prayer of toes.

3.

Fields   sea green at six a. m.
Vert   verde   verdant –
ground mist rolls up the shores of hedgerow.
Mosquitoes brutal.
I swat my head with the map.
   Three deer startle
                    pool their gaze
   high-tail it to safety in the cedars.

4.

I get lost tramping between fields
walk east instead of south
can't find the belfry above the monastery's west wall.
(I'm playing at 'lost and found' with God.)

Not even the tangerine sun sucking light out of evening
knows west this night.

Am I really called by name?

5.

                    I dream of a boy
in a blue helmet   shouting
Stop!   &   Whoa!
Jack-in-a-box   he springs high
draws knees in tight   lands
flat on his back   The pantomime repeats
I try to obey   my bike wobbling
                            rusty brakes –

while all along   a grassy swath leading to woods
has been waiting   its poured brightness
marred though by a barren tree
                                     crooked arms
                                             outstretched.
A notice board   oozes tears

      Silver rain is falling in the green wood now
and suddenly blinded –
                       I stagger into hands that catch my
  head –
old hands   leather-leaf hands –
  Are you afraid   he asks?
  I sometimes have trouble seeing –
                             I fall forward
into the livid wound that seams his forehead
his untroubled eyes.

6.

I am botanist, bird watcher and shepherd of my soul.
At mass I measure my days by stoles   plum-coloured
with blood-red lining   a silver cross woven over the heart –
the green one for St. Patrick   or perhaps a field
of new rye in winter recalling me now to that circle of
  pines –
the outdoor chapel by the lake.
                             We are cross-legged   chanting –
The Lord is in His holy temple   the Lord is in His holy
  temple
Let all the earth keep silent   before Him

Of course I have always kept track of you as I mapped
Arctic climes with my feet.
                        I have seen how you put

the earth in the sky and the sky in the earth —
                              wonder
easier than belief. When asked here about my relationship to God
I fled —
          yet the silence   between call and response
deep as a well   returns more than my face to me —
thoughts... quieter than rivers   I step out
on a threshold of the already and not yet.

Acknowledgements

Several of these poems have appeared in *Arc Poetry Magazine, The Dalhousie Review, The Fiddlehead, Literary Review of Canada, Grain Magazine* and in *Verse Afire (The Ontario Poetry Society)*. Thanks to *Arc Poetry Magazine* for a *First Honorary Mention* in 2008, and to the editors of *The Best Canadian Poetry in English 2008, The Fiddlehead,* for including "Lookout" on their long list.

For the WW1 section entitled *Paper Wings,* I owe an immeasurable debt to the Flying Logs (1917-1918) of my own father, Capt. Arthur Treloar Whealy R.N.A.S – R.F.C. – R.A.F., DSO & Bar, DFC, M.i.D. No. 3 Naval / 203 RFC, RAF Squadrons. The following books were of great value in drawing me closer to an understanding of the war in the air. For a poetic view of the sky and pure love of flying, thanks to *Sagittarius Rising* by Cecil Lewis (Warner Books, 1936); *They Fought For The Sky* by Quentin Reynolds (Cassell & Company Ltd. London, 1958); *Pilot's Log* compiled and edited from the log, diary, letters and verse of Lt. Leonard A. Richardson, RFC 1917-1918, by Elizabeth Richardson-Whealy. Love and gratitude for my brother Arthur Whealy who loaned me his library, answered countless questions and fueled me with joy in the writing.

Once again, heartfelt thanks to Allan Briesmaster, whose generosity, friendship and editorial vision has guided me over the years of writing this book. Thanks to Don McKay who was instrumental in helping me articulate first ideas at the *Writing With Style* program at The Banff School of Writing in 2005. Thanks too, for deep learning over years in the many classes and workshops I have taken with Bruce Meyer, Al Moritz, Molly Peacock and Ken Babstock. My poetry group has always been unstinting in their enlightened suggestions: special thanks to Sue Chenette, Katy Marshall Flaherty, Susan Helwig, Donna Langevin, Chris Pannell and Phoebe Tsang. Singular thanks goes to George Payerle and Brian Brett whose finishing touches made the difference.

My gratitude goes to Michael Mirolla of Guernica Editions for continued faith in my work, and making this book possible.

About the Author

Rosemary Clewes has been published most recently in *Descant Magazine, Queen's Quarterly, The Dalhousie Review, Grain Magazine, The Fiddlehead* and *Arc Poetry Magazine*. In 2005, she was nominated by *The Malahat Review* for The National Magazine Awards. She was a finalist in the 2006, CBC Literary Awards. In 2008, she published a book of prose and poetry entitled *Thule Explorer: Kayaking North of 77 Degrees*. In 2009, The Bishop Strachan School in Toronto invited her for their annual wilderness experience to Algonquin Park, Ontario, where she introduced 120 students to her book on the Arctic. In 2012, Signature Editions published a book of poetry entitled, *Once Houses Could Fly: Kayaking North of 79 Degrees*. She has made seven trips to the Arctic, travelling by kayak, raft and icebreaker.

Printed in June 2014
by Gauvin Press,
Gatineau, Québec